SOCIAL MEDIA MARKETING TODAY

BY MACARENA TORRES

Copyright - 2020 - All rights reserved.

The content contained within this book may not be reproduced, duplicated, or transmitted without direct written permission from the author or the publisher.

Under no circumstances will any blame or legal responsibility be held against the publisher, or author, for any damages, reparation, or monetary loss due to the information contained within this book.

Either directly or indirectly.

Legal Notice:

This book is copyright protected. This book is only for personal use. You cannot amend, distribute, sell, use, quote, or paraphrase any part, or the content within this book, without the author or publisher's consent.

Disclaimer Notice:

Please note the information contained within this document is for educational and entertainment purposes only. All effort has been executed to present accurate, up-to-date, and reliable, complete information. No warranties of any kind are declared or implied. Readers acknowledge that the author is not engaging in the rendering of legal, financial, medical, or professional advice. The content within this book has been derived from various sources. Please consult a licensed professional before attempting any techniques outlined in this book.

By reading this document, the reader agrees that under no circumstances is the author responsible for any losses, direct or indirect, incurred due to the use of the information contained within this document, including, but not limited to, - errors, omissions, or inaccuracies

TABLE OF CONTENTS

Introduction 5
   There is no shortcut. You have to work with this metaphor 6
   The Endgame? 9
   Effective Social Media Marketing 10

Chapter 01 - Social Media Marketing – An Overview 12
   A Winning Definition 13
   Managing Your Expectations 13
   Social Media Marketing can Build Brands If... 14

Chapter 02 - 8 Reasons Why SM Marketing is Essential 16
   Reason #1: Social media's huge direct and viral reach 16
   Reason #2: Social media is habitual 17
   Reason #3: Target audiences use different content formats 17
   Reason #4: Most social media platforms can be segmented 18
   Reason #5: Sharing content on most platforms can be automated 19
   Reason #6: You can run a two-track marketing campaign using mailing lists 20
   Reason #7: Your brand gets natural repetition through multi-platform marketing 21
   Reason #8: Save money through content re-purposing 21

Chapter 03 - Manage SM Marketing Campaign Depending on Your Online Business 24
   What do you have available? 25
   The Bottom Line: Don't Just Think Links 26

Chapter 04 - The Classic Way to Do Social Media Marketing and Why it is a 29
Waste of Your Time 29
   The Classic Approach to Social Media Marketing 29
   Audiences are Looking for Quality 30
   The Sad Reality 31
   Other Failed Methods 31

Chapter 05 - Steps to Quicker and Easier Modern SM Marketing 34

Chapter 06 - Niche Research and Targeting it the Right Way 36
   Pick Your Target Niche 37
   List Out Your Niche Indicators 39

Chapter 07 - Your secret Social Media Marketing Weapon: Content Curation 40
   What is Content Curation? 40
   The Best Part 43
   High Attention to Detail is the Key 43

Chapter 08 - Reverse Engineer Your Competitors' Top Content 45
   Focus on What Works 46
   Learn from Your Own Success 47
   The Bottom Line 48

Chapter 09 - Fine Tune Your Payload Content 49

  Study High Click-Through and High Engagement Content Closely 50

  Using the Information Above, Create Payload Content 51

Chapter 10 - Market Your List Right 53

  Finding Out What to Use as an 54

  Incentive 54

  Position All Your Original Content to Push Your Mailing List First 55

  Set Up Your Squeeze Page for Maximum Social Appeal 57

  Set Up the Right Confirmation Page 58

Chapter 11 - Unlock the Power of Repurposed Content 59

Chapter 12 - Use Automatic Content Sharing 62

  Special Notes for Twitter 64

  Special Notes for Facebook 64

Chapter 13 - Scale Up Your Targeting 66

  Experiment with Tagging Niche-Focused Influencers 66

  Experiment with Paid Traffic 68

Chapter 14: Sell to Your List Differently 70

  Use Different Content on Your List 70

  Use Premium Content 72

  Upsell, Upsell, Upsell 72

  Use the $1 List Filtration Method 75

Chapter 15 - Reinvest Your Profits the Right Way 78

  Move into Other Niches after You Master Your System 78

  Buy More Targeted Traffic after You Find Out What Works 79

  Invest in More Original Content 80

  Invest in More Content Updates 80

  Invest in Your Original Products 81

  Sell Your Own Video-Based Membership courses 82

Conclusion 84

Introduction

A lot of marketers have all sorts of wrong ideas about social media marketing. Some think that you only need to post "viral content" to get tons of traffic overnight. They actually believe that if you are able to pump that much traffic to your target website, a large chunk of those people will buy whatever it is that you are selling.

Maybe you're selling services, maybe you're selling an event, or maybe you are selling products from an online store, it doesn't matter. According to this idea, you just need to have a lot of traffic; courtesy of viral content on social media, and you will get the conversions you're looking for.

There is an assumption that social traffic, regardless of which platform it comes from and regardless of how you qualify that traffic, converts to sales readily. Sadly, none of these assumptions are true. In fact, all of them are tragically mistaken.

If you believe in any of these, don't be surprised if you spend a lot of time, effort, and money only to end up with a whole lot of nothing. Welcome to the club.

Effective social media marketing can be reduced to one metaphor. Master this metaphor and you probably will make money on autopilot with social media traffic. Screw up this metaphor or remain clueless to it, and you'll continue to struggle; you'll continue to believe that social media traffic can easily be generated through viral content. You might keep running after that unicorn only to get tired and frustrated.

It doesn't have to be this way. You just have to have the right metaphor or the right conceptual model to make social media marketing work for you. Best of all, you can make it work on autopilot.

You probably have heard of all sorts of "set it and forget it" systems. You probably bought at least one of these products. Well, they're definitely on the right track as far as their label. Social media marketing can be automated. It can be mastered to the point where it can produce income after you've set it. But getting there is another matter entirely. And that's the price people have to pay.

And unfortunately, most people are not willing to pay for that. They're excited about shortcuts, but they're not willing to take the stairs to get to the top. At the back of their minds, they're thinking that there has to be some sort of elevator.

There is no shortcut. You have to work with this metaphor

What am I getting at? Well, the secret to effective social media marketing is an inverted pyramid. It looks like a funnel. That is the metaphor you should have in your mind when thinking of ways to get traffic from social networks and  social media platforms and turning that into cold, hard cash in your bank account.

I need you to keep this idea of an inverted pyramid in your mind. It should have a wide base at the top. The top of that pyramid is heavy visibility. It has to be there. You need to be visible on the four major social media platforms. I'm talking about Facebook, Twitter, YouTube, and Pinterest.

Taken together, the traffic volume you can get from these four platforms is mind-blowing. They can potentially pump a tremendous amount of traffic. But that's just part of the equation. That's just the top of the funnel. Potentially, you can push a lot of traffic from the top. That's how wide the top of the funnel is.

This training will focus on these four platforms, but you can pretty much use the tips that I'm going to share with you and modify them to market on other platforms since many of these principles easily apply.

You might need to modify them a little bit. For example, if you are thinking of marketing on Instagram, a lot of the things that I will teach you about Facebook, Twitter, YouTube, and Pinterest, can be tweaked to work well on the Instagram platform.

Now that you have a clear idea of the heavy visibility that you can achieve with social media, keep in mind that visibility does not mean traffic or clicks to your site. This is a myth. The visibility that I'm talking about means visibility on those platforms.

When people share your content within those platforms, you can enjoy a tremendous reach within such platforms.

But this does not automatically mean that when you share content on Facebook, people who see your link on the materials shared by their friends would automatically click them.

Get the idea out of your head that raw visibility, or as Facebook terms it, "reach," automatically translates to traffic. It doesn't work that way. Instead, you need to start with heavy content visibility on each platform. People must see your stuff there. You must achieve a wide enough reach.

People may not necessarily click on through to your site, but that's secondary. At this point, you just want your brand to be visible. You just want people to become familiar with your brand.

So what's the big deal about visibility anyway? You may be thinking since visibility doesn't mean actual visitors to your website, what good is it?

Think about it this way, when was the last time you saw an ad for the first time and automatically clicked it? If you're like most other people, you probably would want to see the ad show up a few times for you to become familiar with it. You might glance at it from time to time, you might read the description from time to time, but after enough showings, you might seriously think of clicking through.

The same applies to your content on social media platforms. Don't expect that just because you come up with catchy titles and nice, attention-grabbing graphics that this is enough for you to expect a tremendous amount of clicks to your website. It doesn't work that way.

People have to be comfortable enough. Your content has to become familiar enough for them to click on it.

When audience members click on the content you share through your social media accounts, they get a chance to like your page, follow your Twitter feed, pin your posts, or subscribe to your YouTube channel. They still stay on the platform, but they get a chance to subscribe to your account or follow you.

This is the second stage of the social media funnel or inverted pyramid. You have to develop some sort of in-platform credibility. Your content is not just this random material that came out of nowhere. Even if people don't click on it, they see enough similarity in terms of branding, graphics, as well as other content cues so that your brand stands apart from everybody else's.

Again, they may not necessarily be motivated to click, but with enough repetition through social media channels targeting certain topic categories and hashtags, your brand doesn't remain an unknown quantity.

Once you have people checking your content out through your social media accounts, you can then send them "call to action" content (CTA). This content recruits people to your mailing list. This social content that you're sharing offers some sort of incentive.

Maybe you're giving away a free booklet, maybe you're giving away software—whatever the case may be, there is some sort of giveaway to incentivize people to click on that link, enter their email address, and join your mailing list.

Whether you use freebies, special content, special free tickets to an online webinar that's pre-recorded, it doesn't really matter. Whatever the case may be, the endgame is to get people to join your list.

The Endgame?

When you look at the funnel, the endgame is to get people to that narrow end of the funnel. At that end, you're not necessarily getting them to click on an ad to buy something. You're doing something far more valuable.

Instead, you're calling them to action so they join your list. You are converting your social media reach, meaning, the top end of the funnel, to list membership, which is at the very narrow point at the bottom of the inverted pyramid.

This is where the magic happens. Once people join your list because you have successfully incentivized them to enter their email on your squeeze page, you get a tremendous opportunity to build a long-term sales relationship.

That's really the best way to describe it because when people give you their email addresses, what they're really telling you is that they trust you enough to want to have a business relationship with you.

This means you should not abuse that relationship. You should not send them garbage. You should not send them spam. And by spam, I'm talking about material that is not related to the topic of your list.

Stay on message. Because if you are able to do this, you would have a tremendous opportunity to shape the conversation and continue to sell and convert your list, not just once, not just twice, but over the long haul.

Many successful list marketers make seven figures every single year, and all they have is a mailing list. It all depends on how you build that list, who is on that list, and what you are selling on that list.

Regardless of how you cut it, you can turn what would otherwise be a huge amount of social media reach into a loyal list. This is the secret to effective social media marketing.

You probably haven't heard this before. I would not be surprised because the vast majority of social media marketing books out there trying to trick you into thinking that you just need to harvest all this traffic from social media so people can click like monkeys on the ads on your website.

Maybe that worked when Facebook 1st launched nationally. It definitely doesn't work today. Sadly, this is where too many marketers fail. They screw this up.

Now that you know the secret, here's some bad news. This is precisely the point where too many marketers screw up. When they're sending social media content, they promote their squeeze page directly. Although the squeeze page gives away freebies and incentivizes people to sign up, this is too much too soon.

And, not surprisingly, a lot of these marketers burn through a lot of exposure just to get people to their list. Worse yet, when these people join their mailing list, they're completely unprepared. They don't know what to expect, they're not properly conditioned, a lot of them are not even fully qualified to become list members.

So what do they do? They end up doing a whole lot of nothing. This is actually the worst kind of list member.

It's much better to just have a very tiny list because if you have a huge list and almost everybody doesn't do anything to put money in your pockets, you're going to be paying for those list squatters month after month.

Alternatively, you might attract list bouncers. These are people who join your list just to get whatever premium you're offering, download it, and then promptly unsubscribe. They have effectively bounced from your list.

Effective Social Media Marketing

Effective social media marketing means using your social media traffic and highly effective content shared on social media to build successful relationships. Your email list is going to be the platform you will use to convert the relationships made possible through all that social media traffic.

You're essentially creating highly targeted mailing lists using content shared on targeted channels on social media. This is the secret to effective modern social media marketing.

Chapter 01 - Social Media Marketing – An Overview

There's a lot of misconceptions regarding what social media marketing actually is. In fact, when you come across people who call themselves social media marketing consultants or practitioners, chances are very high that they will give you different definitions.

Part of this is due to the fact that there are many different points of emphasis when it comes to social media marketing.

Some people focus on the content, others pay more attention to the network that the content is going to be addressed to, others give more of their focus to social engagement. Naturally, to the layperson, social media marketing is a big question mark.

I understand if you're confused at this point. In fact, you may be so confused that you try to simplify things in your head and end up focusing on how to get as much traffic for as little effort as possible.

That is precisely how a lot of online entrepreneurs and marketers approach social media marketing. Sadly, that is a one-way ticket to failure or disappointment. It's not just going to work out sooner or later. With any kind of project, you have to have the right definition, otherwise, you are making things harder on yourself.

Depending on the definition you go with, you might have all sorts of expectations, and if these outcomes do not come to pass, your resolve and your motivation levels start to suffer. You have to work with the right definition.

A Winning Definition

With all of the above said, what is social media marketing for our present purposes? Well, since this training uses list marketing as its main vehicle for converting social media reach into cold, hard cash, social media marketing is all about content-based audience relationship building. Let me repeat that, social media marketing is all about content-based audience relationship building.

You need to use content in a strategic way. You need to speak to certain audiences and build a relationship with them. This relationship is not this broad word that makes people feel good but ultimately doesn't mean much of anything. Instead, this relationship has a tangible form. And I am, of course, talking about your mailing list. Once you get people on your mailing list, that's when the fun begins.

Everything else is just a workup or a preliminary prior to that point. You need to get people on your list. Social media marketing is going to be your primary vehicle to get people to your list. Everything has to revolve around that list. And this must shape, inform, and guide your social media actions.

Managing Your Expectations

A content-based audience relationship approach to social media marketing sets different expectations compared to other ways of defining this type of marketing. When you read the typical social media marketing book, for example, "How to Dominate Twitter," the focus in on traffic.

13

Unfortunately, if that is your main goal, you end up with a "the more the better" mindset and you feel really depressed at the end of the day because the traffic doesn't come. Even if it does, there's not going to be enough of it. You *have* set yourself up to fail.

When you use a content-based audience relationship-building approach to social media marketing, your focus is on getting the right content in front of the right eyeballs to build the right levels of trust.

This is a long term game. It is definitely a marathon and not a sprint. Since that is your expectation coming in, you position yourself for long term victory. You're not going to be the typical failed social media marketer who jumps into the game with both feet only to find out that the traffic simply isn't there. So what do they do? That's right, they quit.

Manage your expectations by focusing on the right definition and you will be okay. The worst thing that you can do right now is to sabotage any chance of future success by defining the problem the wrong way and filling your mind with all the wrong expectations.

Social Media Marketing can Build Brands If...

Now that we've defined social media marketing, the next step is to focus on the end result of this content-based audience relationship-building approach. If you do everything right, you walk away with a brand. Let me tell you, that is the best asset you will ever have.

Now, in terms of real-world traffic, you may get a low to moderate level of traffic. But if you build a solid brand, that traffic is all you need. That is qualified traffic. These are not random people just blindly clicking on links out of curiosity. These are people who are actually interested in whatever it is you are trying to sell. They want to truly learn more.

They want to build a relationship with you because they want to know what you're about, like what you have to offer, and eventually trust whatever it is you are pushing. These are real people. And this is only possible if you build a solid brand. You have to deliver solid value.

I wish I could tell you that content marketing is enough to do it. I really wish that I can say that, but that is not true. That only explains part of the situation. Sure, you have to deliver content that people truly are interested in, but at the end of the day, when they join your list, they are expecting and deserve value.

That's how you build a solid brand. When people join your list, they will quickly find out that they did not waste their time because you send high-quality updates that actually add value to their lives. Social media marketing can explode the rate at which brands are formed. That's why a lot of people are ranting and raving about social media marketing, but a lot of them are clueless as to how to build a solid brand. Most of the time, they just stumbled into it.

I've let you in on the secret. It's all about content-based audience relationship building. There are many different parts to that equation, and I'm going to walk you through them in a practical way in the following chapters. In this section, I just want you to wrap your mind around the definition and the expectations that flow from it. This is how we tightly define the project that you are going to embark on.

Anything less, chances are, you're going to beat yourself up unnecessarily because you just had unrealistic expectations. This is not one of those get rich quick schemes. This is not one of those overnight success stories. This requires real work. This is the real deal. Are you ready for the journey? Great. Let's go on to chapter 2.

Chapter 02 - 8 Reasons Why SM Marketing is Essential

Just to be sure, if you are in any way, shape, or form unclear as to the value of social media marketing, here are just 8 reasons why it needs to be part of your comprehensive online marketing plan. Maybe your current plan puts more emphasis on search engine marketing, maybe you're currently focused on outreach—those are all well and good.

But to really round things out and add a lot more value to your current online marketing campaign, social media marketing has to be part of the equation. It doesn't have to take center stage, it doesn't have to be your overarching priority, but it has to be part of the total mix. Here are just 8 of the thousands of reasons why your company, regardless of its size, needs to do social media marketing.

Reason #1: Social media's huge direct and viral reach

If you build a solid page on Facebook, you develop a direct reach. This means that a certain percentage of people who like your page will see your updates. While it is true that Facebook has been reducing the organic reach of Facebook pages

recently, there's a workaround to that. When people go to your page, you can instruct them to like your page and then click your page's setting to show your updates first.

You might want to show a video that teaches people how to do this. You might even post an animated gif. Whatever you do, clue people in that they can fix their settings to see your updates first. Now, for people to take the time and bother to do this, you have to offer really valuable content. This puts the onus on you. There has to be real value on your page for them to want to do this. But you can increase your direct reach by instructing people.

On top of that, when people like your content, they can share it on their wall. Since people on Facebook have friends and their friends have friends, this can easily have an exponential effect. In fact, even if your page only has a hundred likes, but these are real people with real friends, don't be surprised if one of your posts gets really viral and spreads all over the place.

Social media enables you to have a large direct reach. It also provides you with a tremendous opportunity to enjoy exponential content coverage.

Reason #2: Social media is habitual

While different demographics have shown the softening or weakening of social media usage on a daily, weekly, or monthly basis, this still doesn't take away from the fact that a lot of people habitually use social media. In fact, a lot of people do this the first thing in the morning.

When they wake up, they go to their mobile phone or tablet and check their updates. It can easily become a habit. This gives you a tremendous opportunity to get your content and brand in front of many interested eyeballs.

Reason #3: Target audiences use different content formats

The great thing about social media marketing is that you're not restricted to just one content format. You're not restricted to video, pictures, links, blog posts, text, or audio files. Instead, different platforms specialize in different formats. And when you create content for one platform, you can easily make different versions of it in different formats to spread out to other platforms.

For example, I write a blog post and post it on Facebook. I create a very attention-grabbing graphic for that blog post. So when I post it on my Facebook page, a preview of the image shows up and it grabs a lot of attention. People click on it, and they end up on my website.

I can take that graphic and share it on Pinterest. I can take the text of my blog post or article and create a slideshow video out of it and share it on YouTube. I can also take the video and embed it on my blog post. I can strip different parts of the article or post itself and feed it into Twitter along with the link to the full post or article.

Do you see how this works? You get access to the different audiences of those different platforms by simply re-purposing or recycling the same content that you made for one platform and sharing those other formats on other platforms. This increases your potential reach.

Reason #4: Most social media platforms can be segmented

If you've ever been to Instagram, you know that when you see a picture, it usually has many different tags. If you've been on Twitter, you'd see that a lot of the hot tweets also have hashtags. Those tags are very valuable. When you use a tag with your content, you are essentially categorizing your content. People use those tags to search for content. This is a very powerful segmentation tool.

People who are looking for cute Chihuahua puppies will use certain hashtags that are different from people looking for libertarian political posts. If you have a very tightly defined audience, social media platforms' built-in segmentation tools and features can definitely help you.

You probably already know that huge audiences that are not very targeted are essentially worthless. Thanks to social media marketing's segmentation features, you can get a smaller volume of people from many different platforms, but you can rest assured that these people are actually interested in whatever it is you are saying. These segmentation tools go a long way in helping you build a very refined and well-qualified audience base. This, in turn, increases your likelihood of making a sale.

Reason #5: Sharing content on most platforms can be automated

Thanks to tools like Hootsuite and SocialOomph, you don't have to worry about manually going to Facebook or Twitter and copying and pasting materials from a document or spend hours setting up your scheduled posts. You can automate your posts to publish up to six months on Facebook. This means that you can set up your Facebook account to post six to ten or more times every day, but you don't have to babysit it because you have fed the content in.

The best part is that a lot of these automation tools use bulk feeds. Meaning, you can format your content in an Excel file and convert it to CSV, and plug into these tools. You don't have to input the materials one by one. Talk about saving a lot of time while also maximizing your reach.

Reason #6: You can run a two-track marketing campaign using mailing lists

The heart of a content-based audience relationship marketing campaign on social media is to build a highly targeted mailing list. Now, this is not what you think. A lot of people are thinking that once they build the list, they're on their way to becoming millionaires. Absolutely wrong. There's a missing step.

When people join your mailing list, it really is a "general" mailing list. By "general," I'm not saying that it talks about all subjects under the sun. I'm not talking about that. Instead, I'm talking about general interest in the specific topic. You really don't know yet at this point who is a buyer and who is a person who is simply looking for information and is still trying to make up their minds whether they trust you enough.

You create a general list and then eventually you try to upsell them to a buyer's list.

How do you do that? Well, you sell low-cost items on your general list. You can sell a booklet for $1. It doesn't really matter what the price is. It has to be very low because what you're really trying to do here is that you're trying to give people a means to identify themselves as a buyer and you want to make it as smooth and easy as possible. A dollar is almost an afterthought to most people.

They won't think that it's too painful to buy your product. But once they get to your buyer's list, you eliminate them from your general list, and now you have a pure list of buyers. That list, my friend, is a goldmine. That's where you send your money-making updates. That's where you get people to check out your case studies and get them to pay top dollar for whatever affiliate programs or original products you are pushing on your buyer's list.

This is called a two-track marketing campaign. It's extremely powerful and it has made a lot of people rich. But you have to step away from the very common mistake of thinking that once you get a lot of people to your mailing list, you have it made. Absolutely wrong. There is another step that you need to take.

Reason #7: Your brand gets natural repetition through multi-platform marketing

Assuming that all your social media accounts on all four major platforms look similar to each other, you get many bites at the apple. You really do. When people run into your brand on Facebook, there's a chance they might run into your brand on Twitter.

If there is enough graphical similarity between your brands, then they can see that you're all over the place and they can converse or engage with your brand regardless of where they are on the internet.

Eventually, this builds a tremendous amount of familiarity, and people might become so comfortable that they join your mailing list when you call them to action. The best part of this is that it happens naturally by you simply creating accounts on all the major platforms. Your brand speaks to people who are interested in your niche, regardless of where they go.

Reason #8: Save money through content re-purposing

Make no mistake about it, content generation is expensive. Even if you

hire highly qualified, talented, skilled, and experienced people from countries with huge numbers of people who speak English as a second language, you can still be out thousands of dollars every year. High-quality writers from places like India, Pakistan, and the Philippines may be cheaper than American writers, but their costs still add up over time.

One of the things about social media marketing that really excites me is the fact that you can create content and re-purpose it into many different formats. This reduces your cost.

If I hire a writer from India and pay that person $1,000 a month, I can get a fixed amount of content. At this point, I can choose to pay that person another $1,000 to get even more content, or I can take whatever content he or she produced and turn them into videos, infographics, or strip them down into questions for tweets.

I can turn them into diagrams, I can take the voice-over of the video that I produced and turn it into a sound file. I can even make a slideshow of these materials. Once I have all these re-purposed content, then I can share them on format-specific platforms. For example, I can share the slideshows on Slideshare. I can post the infographics on Pinterest.

I can post product shots or general product pictures on Instagram. I can post the questions on Twitter. I can also post the videos on YouTube. Best of all, I can post all the formats on Facebook. Do you see how this works? When you do this, you buy content once, re-purpose it, and share it so you get a higher chance of getting traffic or visibility with that re-purposed content.

You're not creating content constantly. In fact, the name of the game is to produce as little content as possible, but market these high-quality pieces widely. This is how you maximize their value. The old idea of constantly publishing content just to get a few eyeballs here and there is dead. Seriously. That's a one-way ticket to the poorhouse.

Your better approach would be to make that content work for you by converting it into many different formats.

You then share these different formats on platforms that specialize in those formats. I hope the 8 reasons above are clear and that you are pumped up to do social media marketing right. In chapter 3, we're going to talk about picking a social media marketing campaign that is most likely to produce results for your type of online business. See you there.

Chapter 03 - Manage SM Marketing Campaign Depending on Your Online Business

I know this chapter is going to throw a lot of people off, but people need to understand this. One of the major reasons why a lot of otherwise intelligent and experienced social media marketers fail to get the results that they're looking for is the fact that they're using the wrong approach. Their approach to social media marketing and the websites they're promoting is a one-size-fits-all approach.

Now, you don't need me to explain to you why that is a bad idea. It doesn't work in most areas of your life and it definitely doesn't work when it comes to social media marketing. You can't look at this project with the mindset that as long as you pull traffic from social media platforms, then you can use the exact same method and the exact same communication tactics, regardless of the online entity or business you are promoting.

Since we're using content to develop relationships on social media platforms, this one-size-fits-all approach is even more fatal. I mean, it's a bad enough idea as it is, but if you were to use a content-based campaign, it gets even worse. The reality is that different business types require different content and publishing strategies. You have to customize, modify, and tweak your particular content and publishing strategies on social media to fit the type of website you are trying to promote.

Now, there are a huge number of website variations out there. In fact, there are too many. I would venture to say that the only limit, really, is your imagination. But if you were to categorize these different website types into four rough forms, they would more or less fall into the following: publishing, e-commerce or drop shipping, email lists, and traffic sales.

Again, there are many variations of these, but if you were to look at the different *types of* business*es* out there, you can pretty much reduce them to these four types. When you study these closely, they have different needs. They have different features that must be addressed, otherwise, you're not going to get the results you're looking for.

Unfortunately, a lot of social media marketers would try to promote a blog the exact same way they would try to promote a drop shipping or e-commerce website. Similarly, somebody who is essentially just trying to sell their social media traffic is trying to do content marketing like somebody with a blog. It doesn't work. It doesn't make any sense.

The bottom line is obvious: different strategies require different content types. You must start with the type of online entity you are promoting. Are you promoting a blog? Do you have a website that uses a lot of articles? Do people contribute content? Well, you have a publishing website. Do you have a drop shipping online store? Maybe you built it with Shopify and you use Oberlo to get products from Aliexpress.

When people buy stuff from your storefront, your software orders the materials from Aliexpress and you keep the difference. Maybe you sell from your own inventory, it doesn't really matter. You run an e-commerce website. This is very different from a publishing business. Similarly, if you make your money through your mailing list, you can't market on social media the same way as you would if you had an online store. Again, different strategies require different content types.

What do you have available?

Now that I've gotten you thinking about how special your specific website target is, I need you to look at the different content types available to you. You need to think outside the box. You need to look at all the available options out there and how you can create content that

is tailored to your specific type of online entity.

Here is the list of content types you can use to promote different online entities, but your specific focus and specialization should weigh more heavily on certain types of content instead of others:

- ☐ Audio clips
- ☐ Slideshows
- ☐ Infographics
- ☐ Diagrams
- ☐ Blog links
- ☐ Videos

The Bottom Line: Don't Just Think Links

It really freaks me out, in fact, it really saddens me when I see a lot of otherwise capable social media marketers focus almost entirely on spreading their links. They think that is the endgame. Well, yes, links are important. I can see where they're coming from because when people Click on a link, that's instant traffic.

But you have to understand that depending on the type of target site you are promoting, you would build a tighter brand if you share different types of content.

In many situations, you probably would be better off sharing more audio or infographics and diagrams than if you were sharing naked links because people are bombarded with links every single day. You have to pay your dues. You have to become familiar enough with your target audience members using these different content types for them to eventually trust you enough to click on your link.

Unfortunately, a lot of people have this in reverse. They start with the links and when they get desperate, they then use other types of content. At that point, they are a day late and a buck short. Don't do that. Instead, use the derivative content first and then play up the links. Also, not all of these formats work with your particular type of website.

I would suggest that you look at your competitors first and pay close attention to the type of content they are currently sharing. What kind of format do they use? Are they sharing mostly picture quotes? Are they focused primarily on video? Do they have a special fondness for diagrams? This is not random. This is actually telling you all you need to know about how to appeal to your target audience members.

This is no time to "be revolutionary" and come up with something completely out of the left field. That's not going to work. There's a reason why your competitors are not doing that. At this point in the game, you should focus on what everybody else is doing and reverse engineer their formats.

Once you have established a distinct brand, then you can experiment with different formats, different ways of doing things, and possibly come up with something that is distinct to your brand.

But until and unless you reach that point, you need to focus first on reverse engineering what everybody else is doing. In other words, let them do your homework. Focus on what they're doing right and build on it. Figure out their areas for improvement and come up with a more compelling offer. Pay attention to what they're not doing. Avoid those because obviously, it doesn't pay.

I hope I'm being clear here. Make sure that your content types, as well as your sharing strategies, fit the type of business you're in. A little bit of reverse engineering can definitely go a long way.

Chapter 04 - The Classic Way to Do Social Media Marketing and Why it is a Waste of Your Time

Before I jump into the actual meat and potatoes of this training, I need to devote some real estate to how other people are doing social media marketing. I need to do this because it's very tempting for people to engage in the same practices.

I can see where they're coming from. It is easy. It's like seeing some chump change in front of you and it's almost irresistible to fight the urge of bending over and picking up that change.

But when you do that, it will throw you off. It will give you a false sense of incentive or reward and don't be surprised if you end up giving in to your worst instincts only to walk away with less than nothing.

This happens all the time because human beings, being the way they are, would always take the path of least resistance. Who can blame them? But by warning you about how this works out, it is my hope that you stay away from this and focus instead on investing your time, effort, and energy on the right way to do things.

The Classic Approach to Social Media Marketing

So what is the classic approach to social media marketing? Well, it's actually quite simple. Whether we're talking about Instagram, Twitter, or Facebook, you need to only "follow,"

"like" or "friend" people who are interested in your niche.

You connect with all these people, and then after you have followed them, a lot of them would actually follow you back. For example, on Twitter, for every 100 follows, don't be surprised if maybe 20 to 30 people follow you back.

Now, this is where it gets really bad. Classic social media marketers would then spam their followers. They would just send all sorts of unrelated garbage, and then they would unfollow. Do you see the pattern? Follow, get followed, spam, unfollow. And I wish I could tell you that they do this sporadically, but instead, these self-professed "professional marketers" use all sorts of sophisticated software to do this.

Up until a few years ago, this worked like a charm. This was a great way to get a lot of Twitter traffic. But not anymore. This pattern, instead, can get you banned.

More importantly, whatever traffic you do manage to get using this tactic is not going to be any good. Why? There's no targeting. You're not pre-qualifying these people who would follow you.

The only reason why they followed you in the first place is that you followed them first. Where's the selection there? Where is the targeting there? Now, you can make wild guesses, but ultimately, it's a volume game and it leads nowhere. The return on effort is not there.

I'm not saying that you can't make any sales doing this technique. I'm not claiming that. But what I am saying is that whatever rewards you get are not offset by the wasted time, effort, and energy as well as opportunity costs involved. You're better off using a quality-based approach.

Audiences are Looking for Quality

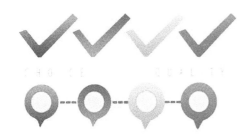

The bottom line to the Social Media Marketing Revolution is to use quality content. Your content will speak for you.

Your content will do the pre-sales job regarding your brand.

In other words, your content is your representative. It speaks *to* the values you *want your* brand to be associated with.

The Sad Reality

Even if the "follow, get followed, spam, and unfollow" technique still works for some people, the rules have changed. Social media platforms will reward or punish you based on engagement. If you want an extreme example of this, just look at Facebook. Facebook used to be a traffic goldmine. Not anymore.

You need a really high level of engagement to preserve your reach on Facebook. If you get normal levels of engagement, good luck. That's how bad things are, and that's why I need to take this time to spell out why this "classic social media marketing" no longer works.

Other Failed Methods

I would be remiss in my duty to educate you on failed social media marketing strategies if I don't also mention other failed techniques. First, hashtag hunting no longer works. This technique involves marketers finding hashtags that are trending. They basically would publish niche-specific content, but use unrelated or irrelevant hashtags and pair them with their content.

They do this because they want to "hitch a ride" on the upward trend of those hashtags. They know people are searching for those hashtags. They know that these hashtag trends are hot, so they want to poach as many eyeballs as possible.

Unfortunately, the traffic that you get is not going to be any good. People are looking for specific types of information, and when they see that your content is so obviously unrelated, they're not going to click through. You might even get reported.

Another failed method you should stay away from is influencer spamming. There are many influencers in almost all niches. If you want to see this in action, go to Facebook or Twitter. There are many specialized pages and specialized Twitter accounts.

Now, constantly mentioning those influencers on your content is not going to help if your content doesn't really add any value. There has to be a reason why you are engaging with these influencers. And drawing their attention is not enough. Getting them to look at your content because you think your content is hot is a lousy idea.

Instead, you should focus your engagement tagging based on what they did. For example, if an influencer was talking about recent trends in athletic shoes, then that person would be fair game for an article I post regarding the latest trends in athletic shoes and what they mean in terms of the bottom line of large footwear apparel companies.

That influencer would be directly interested in what I have to say because I am sharing content that is not only high quality but is directly related to stuff he or she is already talking about. Do you see the specificity here? Do you see the direct link? Now, compare this with an influencer who talks only about forex and I tag that influencer when I'm talking about bitcoin.

That person is going to be annoyed. Do you see the difference? Finally, automated publishing with no outreach is not going to work. Basically, what you're doing is you're throwing spaghetti on the wall and hoping something sticks. If you're just publishing content on an automated basis on Twitter, Facebook, Pinterest, and other platforms, it's anybody's guess whether people would actually engage.

You have to do some outreach. You have to draw eyeballs to your content. You have to find existing pools of highly qualified audiences and get your social media to account in front of their eyeballs.

Use your very best content. If you do this right, your automated publishing on social media will be greatly rewarded. Use a shotgun approach and you're probably going to get the same results as other failed social media marketers.

Chapter 05 - Steps to Quicker and Easier Modern SM Marketing

In this chapter, I'm going to give you an overview of the 10 Steps I'm going to teach you in this training. This training is a product of many failed experiments. Believe me, if you've been exposed to some type of "hot" or "groundbreaking" social media marketing technique or strategy, I've been there. I've done that. This training is a product of all my experiences.

I know what works and I know what doesn't. I also understand that people have different skill levels, time horizons, and project resources. I understand the limitations. I understand most people's concerns regarding social media marketing. Accordingly, I've come up with a 10-Step Program that appeals to most social media marketers, regardless of how small or how big their budget is, and regardless of their skill levels.

If you're looking for a truly effective social media marketing game plan that you can set up to pretty much work on autopilot, this is it. Please understand that these steps that I'm going to layout *are* exactly that. Steps. You need to follow them. You can't skip a step. You can't assume that since I mentioned certain keywords or I'm talking about certain themes and topics that you have mastered this already.

I need you to look at all this information with an open mind and pretend you are learning social media marketing all over again. If you don't have that mindset and you are all too eager to skip steps, don't be surprised if the plan that I'm teaching you will not work for you. How can it? You zipped through it. You rushed. You skipped through certain key parts.

You need to be patient with this program by going through each step. Don't go to the next step until you've mastered the step you're on. I know you're busy, I know you don't have the time, but you need to do this right. Otherwise, you only have yourself to blame if things don't work out. Are we clear? Okay.

Here are the 10 Steps to Faster and Easier Modern Social Media Marketing:

- ☐ Niche research and targeting
- ☐ Content curation
- ☐ Reverse engineer your competition's top content
- ☐ Create fine-tuned payload content
- ☐ Market your mailing list right
- ☐ Unlock the power of repurposed multi-platform content
- ☐ Automate content sharing
- ☐ Scale up your targeting
- ☐ Sell to your list differently
- ☐ Reinvest your profits the right way

Those are the 10 Steps. I know they sound pretty simple. They definitely appear pretty straightforward, but the devil, as always, is in the details. See you in the next chapter.

Chapter 06 - Niche Research and Targeting it the Right Way

I can't even begin to tell you how many times I've run into social media marketers and they automatically want to know about traffic generation. Forget about niche research, forget about consumer intelligence, don't worry about setting up the right site to get in front of the right target audience eyeballs.

Let's just skip straight to the "good stuff." That's the kind of mindset that I run into all the time, and that's why a lot of people struggle in this game.

You have to understand that until and unless you find yourself barking up the right tree, you're just going to be chasing your tail. I know I'm using a lot of dog analogies, but these are the most appropriate. Most people are simply just chasing their tails and wasting a whole lot of time doing stuff that doesn't really add to their bottom line.

A lot of these, and I would guess all of them, can be quickly dispensed with if people only did niche targeting ahead of time. In other words, know your audience. Since you have a clear profile of who your target audience is, the next step is to go to these different social media platforms and find them there.

Believe it or not, whatever it is you are promoting, regardless of how esoteric, obscure or weird it may be, there are already people on social media platforms talking about or showing interest in whatever you are promoting, I know, it sounds crazy, it sounds weird, but it's absolutely true. Your job as a marketer is to find those audiences on these social media platforms.

The way to do this, of course, is to identify your business' target audience. Sadly, most marketers don't even bother with this. Instead, they just look at social media marketing as a simple task of finding traffic. That's it. That's the name of the game.

That's all there is to it. If you want to be successful, you need to be clear about who your target audience is.

And believe me, this is not always easy. You're going to run into the temptation of making "educated guesses" about who your target audience members are. Most of the time, that doesn't work. Thankfully, there is an easier way. The more you take random shots in the dark, making all sorts of wild guesses, the more money and time you will lose.

There is a shortcut here: Find your competitors. Seriously. Just find them. And, let me tell you, regardless of how weird, esoteric, or seemingly "unknown" your niche is, there will at least be one competitor on social media.

Find that organization or business and let them do your niche and target audience research for you. Since they've already started and they are already speaking to your audience, find out who your competitors are and look at their social media profiles.

The reverse engineer who they're following. Pay attention to who they're targeting. Look at how they categorize themselves. In the simplest terms, pay attention to the hashtags they use with their content.

These clues should be enough to give you an idea of where to start. This way, you get a head start. You're not completely stuck in the dark and absolutely clueless as to what to do. Instead, you have some objective tried and proven information you could work with.

Pick Your Target Niche

You have to remember that every business can be positioned in at least one of two ways. The bigger your niche, the more angles you would have at your disposal. You can look at different sub-segments of your niche.

You need to understand how this works because you might think you have a clear niche, but it may well turn out that there are many different layers or tiers to that niche. There might be different subsegments there.

You should have a clear understanding of what your niche is generally, and what subsegments exist within that larger niche. Again, you can reverse engineer your competitors to take a stab at this. Regardless, you need to do this. You need to get this information.

Now that you have an idea of what your target niche is, go to different platforms like YouTube, Facebook, Twitter, and Pinterest. Now, look at whether these places have sizable content areas or messaging areas like Facebook pages, groups, Google Plus communities, Twitter hashtags, Pinterest Pinboards, and existing YouTube channels.

Pay attention to these places and see if your niche is big enough on those different platforms. If you notice that a particular platform doesn't really feature that much content for your specific niche, this is a red flag. The demand may not be there. The audience size might not be worth your while.

On the other hand, if you see there's a lot of videos regarding the topics that you're going to be hitting, this may be a good sign. But you need to do another level of analysis. Pay attention to the number of competitors you have.

If there seems to be a huge number of competitors fighting over the same niche, then this is going to be a problem. But if it turns out that there's a lot of content targeting your niche, but they're only produced by a handful of people or organizations, this is an encouraging sign.

Also, pay attention to how active your target audience members are. Look at the content that's being shared regarding your niche. Do you see a lot of engagement? Do people share this stuff? Is the hashtag quite prevalent?

Look for these and other objective indicators of activity. When you wrap your mind around these indicators, then you should have a clear idea of whether you should target your niche at a particular platform or whether you should ignore a platform altogether.

List Out Your Niche Indicators

While you're doing reverse engineering, pay attention to how your niche is indicated on platforms. These involve hashtags, categories, keyword targets, labeling patterns, and tags. Use these to do the analysis I described above. Again, in any niche, there are sub-niches, so your goal here is to find a sub-niche or a way of positioning your content so you don't run into a ridiculous amount of competition.

You're still tapping into a sizable pool of demand, but you're not making things impossible for yourself by running headlong into the well-entrenched professional competition. You will probably need to keep experimenting with different sub-niches until you find one that is promising enough.

Chapter 07 - Your secret Social Media Marketing Weapon: Content Curation

Now that you have picked the specific sub-niche that you're going to be targeting as well as finished doing advanced research on where your sub-niche or niche segment audiences are located on social media platforms, the next step is to find content.

I've got some good news and some bad news. The good news is that you stand to save a lot of money.

The bad news is that you need to put in a lot more time and pay attention to details. There are no two ways about it. You cannot drop the ball when it comes to the quality of the content that you are going to be sharing on your social media accounts.

Each and every piece of content you share must build your brand. This is nonnegotiable. You can't just pick random pieces of content that somehow, someway, has something to do with your niche.

That's not going to help you get the right eyeballs. That's not going to help you establish the kind of credibility and authority you need to eventually convert highly specific and qualified traffic from social media into cold, hard cash.

What is Content Curation?

As I've mentioned above, you stand to save a lot of money with content curation. This should be obvious. After all, you're not going to be using the content that you yourself created. Content curation is all about picking

other people's content and sharing those materials on your social media accounts. This creates a win-win situation.

Since you're sharing links and descriptions of such content, the creator of that content gets free traffic. You, on the other hand, get to build up your credibility because people are rewarded for following your accounts with highly targeted, highly specific, value-added content.

Everybody wins. The user wins, you win, and of course, the original content creator comes out ahead. This is how it's supposed to work. You win big time because you save a tremendous amount of money not having to create a huge amount of original content.

If you've ever tried to write your own stuff or outsourced content creation, whether in the US or to other parts of the world, it can get quite expensive very quickly.

Content curation enables you to build credibility with your audience in a very inexpensive way. You use other people's content. You get to entertain them, build credibility, and gain their trust. The downside here is the time. Sure, you're not spending greenbacks, but you're definitely going to be spending time.

As I've mentioned above, you cannot be indiscriminate when you are trying to do content curation. Whatever goodwill you have built up for your brand will go up in smoke if people catch on to the fact that you are just randomly curating and spreading low-quality content that may have something to do with your niche. That's not going to cut it. Not by a long shot.

Adopt the Right Content Curation Strategy

Now that you know where your target audience members are on social media platforms, you build credibility by populating your social media accounts with highly credible, high authority third party content.

This is called curation.

In between those materials, you are going to be sharing your own original content. From time to time, you're going to call people to action to take a look at the incentives you're giving away for them to join your mailing list. This is how you play the game.

When people follow you, they are rewarded with top-notch content. It doesn't really matter whether you produced that material or it was written by somebody else, your followers get rewarded for following your account.

They get niche-specific material. Eventually, you build trust with them because you only send them the very best materials. They start paying attention to your own materials. More importantly, they start noticing the content you share, which actively encourages them to sign up for your mailing list.

This is the key. You intersperse your own original content. You create an impression of quality in their minds because you're sending only the very best third party content. You then mix in your own original content which is of the same quality as the other stuff you're sending. Eventually, they warm up to your brand, and this is where your call to action content comes in.

You call them to action regarding the freebies you're giving away. Maybe you're giving away software, a booklet, discount codes, or even a full-blown book, it doesn't matter. You are ethically bribing them to enter their email addresses so they can download the incentive. That's how you build up your mailing list.

On top of all of this, when people join your mailing list, you call them to action to share the emails that you're sending them. Maybe you should ask them to forward that email to their friends. Maybe you would want them to copy and paste the material and post it on their Facebook wall.

The Best Part

The best part of content curation is that it's very easy to automate. Seriously. This is one way of content promotion that is very automation-friendly. You only need to get the URLs of the third-party content that you're curating and plug them into an Excel sheet. You then convert the

file into a CSV file, which is then imported by social media scheduling tools like Hootsuite and SocialOomph.

You don't have to manually enter everything. You don't have to schedule everything by hand. You can do all of this through software. Isn't that awesome? You get to build credibility while at the same time minimizing work.

Now, with that said, you need to pay special attention to content quality.

High Attention to Detail is the Key

You have to resist the temptation of running basic keyword searches on Google or on social media platforms and grabbing anything that is somewhat related to your niche. That is a one-way ticket to brand destruction. You worked hard to build your social media brand, it really would be a shame to see all of that go up in smoke

because the content you're curating is very unpredictable when it comes to quality.

There may be several days where you're sending the very best, cutting edge reports on your niche, followed by a few days of just completely worthless content. What do you think prospective fans would think? Either they would think that your brand is unreliable or you're unprofessional. Whatever the case may be, you're not going to be convincing people that your brand focuses on the very best in your niche.

You need to be very discriminating when you select your content. You have to read through the materials. Make sure that the content is alive, updated, and well-written. This, of course, takes time. The trade-off, obviously, is that you don't have to spend money.

Regardless, you need to pay close attention to the content that you're sharing because it represents your brand. The quality it contains either makes your brand look good or erodes your brand. It's your choice.

Chapter 08 - Reverse Engineer Your Competitors' Top Content

In the previous chapter, I mentioned that you're going to have to mix in your original content. Now, the question that's probably at the top of your mind is, "How do I know which content to produce?"

Well, there are two ways to do this, like I mentioned earlier in this training. You can try to figure things out on your own and engage in all sorts of experiments, or you can just simply allow your competitors to do your homework for you.

I hope you can see which path is the easiest. It should be obvious. If you are sending the very best content on your niche, your original content must be at the same level or better. Otherwise, your followers are not going to take the bait. They're not going to trust your brand.

They appreciate the fact that you're collecting all this information, and they're probably going to stick around and follow your social media accounts, however, you can't count on them to do much of anything else. There's really no incentive for them to join your mailing list.

Why should they? Your content is not that great. They only need to compare the kind of original content you produce with *the* other top-notch third party stuff you're sharing to see your weakness. Do you see the problem here?

You have to produce top content if you want your brand to be credible. Thankfully, this is easier than you think. Simply reverse engineer your competitors.

Look at their most successful stuff. How do you know? Look at the social media indicators of their content. How many "likes" do*es* their top content get? How many "shares?" Is there any other indicator that shows that this content actually has traction?

Maybe you should pay attention to the number of comments for that content. Maybe you would want to run a backlink checker on a piece of content and see how many other blogs or websites link to that piece of content.

This is how you measure the overall success of any single piece of content so you can use it as a "template," if you will, for your own content. I'm not saying you should rip it off, instead, I'm encouraging you to use it as a starting point and come up with something so much better.

Focus on What Works

When you look at your competitors' most social pieces of content, you are basing your own original content on themes and topics that actually work. They have traction with your target audience members. You're not wasting money or time taking wild guesses.

This is one of the most common mistakes social media marketers make. They think that they have the best ideas regarding "hot" content in their niche, so they come up with all sorts of content that they think is just plain awesome, only to fall flat on their faces.

I'm telling you, for every 100 pieces of those types of original content, maybe 10 would gain any sort of respectable traction in your niche. It's too expensive, and it burns too much time. Thankfully, there is a better way. You just need to reverse engineer your competitors' most successful content.

Use that as a starting point. You can adjust them, you can modify them, you can come up with your own variations, but at least you get a head start. At least you're in the ballpark when you start off. You're not just taking random shots in the dark.

Learn from Your Own Success

After you have started curating and mixing in your original content, pay attention to your statistics. They should tell you which of your content gets the most love.

If you notice that a handful of your curated third party content gets a a lot of retweets, shares on Facebook, or any other indication of social media engagement, pay close attention to those pieces of content.

At some level or another, they struck a nerve. They caught your audience members' attention in a very positive way. Find these successful curated pieces of content and create original versions of them.

Similarly, if you have many different original pieces of content, only a handful of them would be really successful. Pay attention to those. Find them. Once you've identified them, create more of them. Focus on the same themes and present similar information in the same way.

The key here is to focus on what works and expand it and grow it. Ditch the stuff that failed. Build on your strengths. Create Derivative Cross-Platform Versions of Your Most Successful Content

Now that you have a clear idea of how to create content that has proven traction, don't just keep reverse engineering it. While you need to continue doing that, you also have to do something else. Create derivative or cross-platform versions.

For example, one particular type of blog post does well on all your social media accounts. Identify its themes, pay attention to its patterns, and come up with another blog post. See if that works.

If you achieve the same level of success, you're on to something. This is not a fluke. This is not a one-time thing. You have struck on a theme that your audience members readily enjoy.

The next step is to take things to a whole other level. Instead of just cranking out yet another blog post, create videos about that theme. Make specialized diagrams. Produce infographics.

Take these materials and share them on social media platforms that specialize in those formats. For example, for blog post URLs, share them on Twitter and Facebook. For videos, share them on YouTube. For diagrams and infographics, share them on Pinterest.

Drilling even deeper, look at your hottest blog posts, and strip out key questions and use these as leads or titles for tweets. Tweet the same content several times over the course of a week. Of course, don't drop it all in one hour, but space them out. Still, when you use the right questions, you become very visible on Twitter. Pair these with the right hashtags.

The Bottom Line

The great thing about content curation is you save a lot of money, but you are also positioning yourself to build on your strengths. You focus on things that you're doing right and figuring them out so you can predictably produce successful content.

Now, this is not going to happen overnight. You have to keep experimenting until you find the right themes that consistently work with your audience.

Chapter 09 - Fine Tune Your Payload Content

As I have mentioned previously, you can come up with your very own content based primarily on the social signals of the top-notch third party materials you are curating. Put simply, when you are going through your research, you will keep coming across certain pieces of content that get a lot of engagement on social media.

These are all the objective indicators you need to understand that you are looking at high quality, high demand content. At that point, you can come up with your own version of that content.

You can use it as a template, so to speak. Another approach would be to just do curation first. You just take all the high-quality third party content with great social signals and put them all on auto-publish on your social media accounts.

You run this curation campaign for several weeks. Soon enough, you will see a pattern. Eventually, you will see that some of these materials get a lot more engagement than others. At that point, you can then come up with your own version.

Personally, I pick my own content using both methods. If I'm in a hurry to get people to sign up for my mailing list, I do the first method. But if I'm unsure about the niche or I'm still trying to feel my way around in terms of understanding my audience, I would stick to the second method. There is really no one right answer. It really all depends on your situation.

The great thing about the second method is that you are picking out your original content strategy based on what actually works in terms of your social media accounts. You have to understand that even though high quality third party content may have a lot of objective social signals, those signals may have been generated in different contexts.

Maybe the original publisher was doing something that you may not be doing. Do you see how this works? Still, you can definitely do the first method if you're in a hurry. But if you have some time to spare, you might want to try the second method. Do curation first, let it run, and then pay attention to your statistics. You should be able to see a pattern.

In fact, based on my experience, content that tends to do well often falls within a narrow range of themes. In fact, in some of my campaigns, almost all the content that got a lot of love from the internet was focused on one question. That's how focused your audience's needs may be.

You should pay attention to the following: look at the engagement of the content and the click-through. A lot of social media marketers drop the ball at this point. They think that it's all about engagement. I'm telling you, regardless of how many likes, shares, or comments a piece of content gets, if people don't click through, those engagement signals are not worth much.

Remember, at the end of the day, you want traffic. That's the whole reason why you're doing this in the first place. Getting caught up in how many shares, likes, or comments you get is not going to do you any good. You have to always pay attention to click through.

There has to be some sort of ratio between total engagement and click through. The higher the ratio of the click-through, the more attention you should devote to a piece of content.

Study High Click-Through and High Engagement Content Closely

Now that you have identified curated content that performs well, the next step is to analyze them with a fine-toothed comb. Ask yourself, what problems are people interested in when they read this piece of content? How are these pieces of content

positioned or presented? Do they use some sort of emotional headline? Do they use subheadings that ask questions? Do they drag the person along, or do they just lay out the information dead center?

Pay attention to cosmetic issues. People do judge a book by its cover and blog posts and articles are no different. How are these materials formatted? Do they

have big pictures? Do they have header pictures? Do they use diagrams? What are they doing exactly?

Once you've answered all these questions and you're comfortable with the answers you got, the next step is to create your own content specification sheet. This is going to be your template.

Now, make sure that you're not just basing it on one successful piece of content. That third party content might be a fluke. The company behind it might just have gotten lucky, and for some reason, that piece of content went viral. That's not going to help you.

You have to base your template on the success of many different pieces of curated content. This way, you can be more confident of the fact that even if you barely comply with all the specifications, you would at least get some decent and positive results.

Using the Information Above, Create Payload Content

Now that you have gotten your template together, you need to create your own high quality, high engagement original content. This content is going to be used to sell people on your mailing list. When they read this content, they're supposed to

get excited about joining your mailing list. This is content that is most likely to be credible and most likely to be shared.

Are you excited? Well, don't get too excited. A lot of people jump in with both feet and they end up sabotaging themselves because the payload content they create looks like an advertisement. That's obvious spam. Nobody's going to trust you with that.

You're obviously trying to pull tricks and play games. That's not going to work. Instead, the content must be informative. Think of it as an infomercial. You're selling something, that much is obvious, but people have to walk away with solid value.

You have to walk that tightrope. There's a thin line between shoving stuff down people's throats and providing solid value without asking for anything in return. You have to come up with a decent compromise between the two.

The bottom line is, whatever you do, the content you produce must be valuable. It must add value to the lives of people reading your materials. That's how you build credibility. That's how you get people to get excited about your mailing list.

Remember, your list is supposed to add value to their lives. It's going to be very hard to give that impression when the content that you share is worthless. I hope you can see that. I'll see you in the next chapter.

Chapter 10 - Market Your List Right

Now that you have figured out your payload content, the next step is to understand what kind of giveaway you're going to have to use to get people to sign up for your mailing list.

In an ideal world, people can see the value you bring to the table. They only need to take a look at the content you share as well as the crucial information they get from your premium content. They see this premium content and they see what you're about, what you have to offer, and why it's such a good idea to sign up for your mailing list.

Unfortunately, things don't work out that way. Even if you have the very best blog posts and articles on your website, people still need a push to sign up for your mailing list. This is where incentives come in.

You're going to offer free high-quality premium content, but you're going to repackage it in a way that people would appreciate. Maybe you put it in a book, maybe you would come up with some sort of cheat sheet or resource sheet, or perhaps you can strip it all down into a booklet or even convert it into software form.

Whatever the case may be, this premium free give away content is going to act as an incentive for people to join your mailing list. They get a copy of whatever it is you are giving away for free in exchange for their email.

I call this an ethical bribe. You're bribing people to sign up for your list. Normally, they wouldn't. Only a very few people would take the time and bother to sign up for your list, regardless of how awesome your blog posts and articles are. That's just the reality.

Finding Out What to Use as an Incentive

I hope you can see the logic behind giving away freebies so people can sign up for your mailing list. People need a push. People need some sort of extra sweetener to get the deal going. They need something extra to get them off the fence and onto your mailing list.

Now, the next step is to figure out what kind of incentive to give away so people would join your mailing list. The good news is, you don't have to start from scratch. You don't have to take wild guesses.

You don't have to take shots in the dark. When you pay attention to your top-performing original content, you should have all the information you need to come up with a compelling incentive.

For example, if you run a gardening blog and you notice that a lot of people click on "share" and otherwise engage with your content on tomatoes, it's probably a good idea to come up with a free giveaway book on how to build your own inexpensive tomato greenhouse. Do you see how this works?

Pay attention to your best performing original content. Look at the questions they answer and look at the questions they fail to answer. This way, you can use your popular content as a launching area for your incentive content.

You let your readers know that if they need more information, and they will because the content that they're enjoying is missing certain items, they should click on this link. That link, of course, is your squeeze page. The squeeze page advertises your giveaway and lists out the reasons why people would want to download that giveaway. It's pretty straightforward. You're just offering premium content that your other freely available content is already pointing to.

They're pointing to that content because they don't contain that material. They do a good job building credibility and authority. They do a great job adding value to the lives of your readers, but it's also obvious that certain parts are missing. For those extra materials, they have to sign up. It's absolutely free. It doesn't cost them a dime, but they need to sign up for your mailing list.

This is how you set up your mailing list. It has to be closely tied to your premium content. Coming up with incentives or freebies that look like they came out of the left-field because they're unrelated to whatever it is you're currently doing is not a good idea. Chances are quite good that you're going to fail. When you come up with incentive content that is directly related to the materials you're already sharing, you create a feeling of value. There's also a feeling of exclusivity.

After people have seen your content and have become aware of what you are and what your brand is about, you let them in on a special premium. This is a special deal that other people who haven't accessed your brand have no idea about.

Position All Your Original Content to Push Your Mailing List First

play up the value of your incentive To content, you first have to promote the value of the mailing list. I know this sounds counterintuitive, but if you think about it, it makes all the sense in the world because, in reality, it's the mailing list they're signing up for.

The freebie that you're giving away is just a bribe. It's intended to get people to enter their email address and nothing more. If you were to use all your original content to play up the fact that people can get this additional content, don't be surprised if people sign up to your list and quickly unsubscribe because they really don't care about your list.

Again, you are walking a tightrope here. On the one hand, you want people to get excited about the premium you're giving away for free in exchange for their email address. On the other hand, you want people to see the value that they would get by being members of your mailing list.

This is how you should play it. All your original content should push your mailing list first. I'm not saying that you should not tie it into the incentive, but your original content should highlight the fact that when people join your mailing list, they will continue to get valuable information. This is the key.

Because when you use your tried and proven content to push mailing list membership, people are less likely to join your list and immediately unsubscribe. They are aware of the value that the list can possibly bring to their lives.

You then play up the premium content as part of the membership. In other words, it's an extra. It is not the main focus of the list. Keep the list separate from the premiums you use to get people to sign up to your list.

I hope this is clear because you want to play up the list first, but it must be obvious that you are using the premium content, whether it's a free book, a booklet, a cheat sheet, some sort of pre-recorded video, or something else, as a means to get people to make a decision.

That's the bottom line. You want the incentive to push people to make a decision to join your list, but all your original content, and your website by extension, should push the reader to see the value of being a list member.

A lot of social media marketers completely blow this. They think that it's all about marketing the incentive. Well, to continue with the example I raised earlier, what happens after you get people to sign up to your list in exchange for the greenhouse guide? That's right, nothing.

Why? You played up the value of the greenhouse guide to such an extent that people are clueless as to what other value they would get from the mailing list. Indeed, don't be surprised if people start reporting your list as spam after you start sending them updates.

They were so focused on getting the free book that the updates from your mailing list completely took them by surprise. This happens all the time because of faulty messaging on your blog or website.

You cannot afford to play the game this way. You worked hard to pull all this social media traffic to your site. You spent a tremendous amount of time, effort, and resources to build a solid brand. Unfortunately, you're dropping the ball if you market your mailing list this way.

You must sell the list first, but the incentive must be used to push people to make a decision. This is the proper order of priority. Anything else will fail.

Set Up Your Squeeze Page for Maximum Social Appeal

As I mentioned earlier, you should use your content to push your mailing list. You should use your content to upsell your squeeze page. But this doesn't mean that you can get away with badly designed squeeze pages. That's not going to cut it. Your squeeze page must be well designed. After all, this page is a specialized recruitment page.

When people get on this page, you have to make the case as to why they should join your list, and not just for the incentive. While the incentive takes a big chunk of the real estate of a squeeze page, you should be clear about the fact that people are signing up for your list.

With that said, you have to make your case. Why should people bother with your updates? Why should people stay on your mailing list? What kind of value would they get?

Remember, people are always asking, "What's in it for me?" Your squeeze page must answer that question effectively, clearly, and powerfully. Your squeeze page must be well designed enough to be able to make that connection, while at the same time, it must be easy to market on social media.

Maybe you should have a graphic on your squeeze page that can be easily posted on Pinterest. Maybe you should have a video on your squeeze page that can easily be shared on YouTube.

There are many ways you can go with this. What's crucial is that your squeeze page must be social media-ready. At the same time, it should also do a good job of recruiting people.

Set Up the Right Confirmation Page

When people join your list, thank them and make them feel welcome. You also have to clue them in regarding the content they should expect to receive.

Make them feel that they just did the right thing. Make them feel that they solved a major problem. Not only do they get access to the digital freebie you're giving away, but they're also going to be receiving valuable information regarding a particular topic that they have problems with.

This is how you sell the list. Simply hyping up and over-promoting the premium is not going to help you convert social media traffic into cash. That's just not going to happen. You have to sell the list. You have to build trust in the list.

Chapter 11 - Unlock the Power of Repurposed Content

I've already described this in an earlier chapter, but this topic is so important it deserves its own standalone chapter. When you create original content for your blog or website, you already know that this content has some sort of traction in your niche. You already know that there is a significant amount of demand for this particular type of content.

Not only did you base your decision on the social signals of your reverse-engineered competitor's content, but you're also picking out content choices based on your own statistics. In other words, you're basing your best content on tried and proven material.

You're not taking shots in the dark, you're not taking wild guesses, you're not crossing your fingers and hoping that something sticks.

Instead, you have based your decision on what actually works. Congratulations. But you shouldn't stop there. Once you have noticed that this content really performs based on the number of clicks as well as *the* social media engagement it gets, the next step is to repurpose that content. Turn them into *other* types of content, and re-share them on platforms that specialize in those content types.

For example, if your blog post is getting a lot of retweets and clicks, you might want to strip the blog post into questions. This isn't all that hard because if you look at any type of content, it consists of answers to questions. The questions may not be obvious, the questions may not be plainly stated, but the content is meant to address certain concerns. These concerns can be reworded into questions.

Strip your most powerful and best-performing content into a series of questions. Each question then is linked to the article or blog post that answers it. Tweet these and pair them with niche-specific hashtags.

By using automation tools, you can rotate different questions that essentially promote the same piece of content. Since you're rotating hashtags, there's a high chance that different people looking for different segments of your niche would become aware of your tweet and possibly click through.

Another thing you can do is turn your article into slideshows. Each article brings to mind many different mental images. Come up with different pictures for each of the topics raised by your article and create a simple slideshow using PowerPoint. Share these PowerPoint presentations on Slideshare. You can also use other tools to create a video from your slideshows. Once you've created these videos, you can obviously share them on YouTube.

Alternatively, you can look through the issues you raised in your blog post and turn them into infographics. Infographics are essentially stripped down graphical forms of articles or blog posts. They focus on the most important points you raised and make them easier to understand by the viewer by converting them into pictures. Share these infographics on Pinterest.

Finally, you should make sure that all your blog posts or articles have a nice header picture. This way, when you load the link on Facebook, a nice preview shows up. It grabs eyeballs and people are excited to share the content.

On Facebook, you have a wide range of content formats to choose from. You can share links, videos, infographics, photos, diagrams, and even audio files. After you share materials on your Facebook page, you should then get the link to that post and then share that Facebook page link in Facebook groups that cater to your niche or a related niche.

This is how you unlock the power of re-purposed content. If you play the game this way, you spend less time creating content and more time promoting. Promotion is the name of the game. You may have great content, but it's not going to do you much good if people don't even know it exists. For every hour you spend creating content, you should spend 10 hours promoting that piece of content.

This is how you build up a successful mailing list. This is how you create a solid brand on social media. Start with powerful content, but create different versions and spread it on many different social media platforms.

Chapter 12 - Use Automatic Content Sharing

Before I get into content sharing automation, I want to highlight one other important reason why you should repurpose your content. If your audience members keep seeing that you talk about the same stuff over and over again, chances are, you will lose them.

People want to hear new stuff. People want you to explore other related needs of theirs. They don't want you to basically keep recycling the same stuff over and over again. Unfortunately, that's precisely the kind of risk you're running if you simply focus on giving people more of the same successful stuff.

You know that a particular content theme works. You know it gets a lot of engagement. You know that it draws a lot of clicks. It's perfectly natural for you to want to keep recycling that same theme. Don't do it.

Focus on the very best way to present that theme and stick with that. Just do it a few times, but focus more on re-purposing. This way, when people get into contact with your content, they can see that you are talking about something that appeals to them, but in different formats. They are more likely to pay attention to. They're more likely to click through. They're more likely to share.

Keep this in mind when it comes to re-purposing. Don't think that chapter 11 is completely optional. It isn't. You want your social media feeds to consist of highly successful content as much as possible.

It really would be a shame to figure out what works, only for you to get lazy and just focus on text content. I'm sorry to say it, but text content can only take you so far. Which brings me to content sharing automation. Since you're going to be sharing a lot of content, and much of this content being thridded party as well as original and re-purposed content, you're probably going to have your hands full if you decide to do this manually.

First of all, since you're going to be covering many different platforms and sharing different formats on those platforms, you have a lot of forms to fill *out* over and over again. Sure, you may have created an account once for each of those platforms, but submitting to those places require you to fill in forms. Posting on Facebook involves form filling.

Now, if you really don't have that much content to share, this should be barely manageable. But if you are looking to maximize your visibility by publishing on your social media accounts several times a day, you need to automate.

Unfortunately, simply plugging in information into content publishing tools is not going to do you much good. You have to know when to publish.

Believe it or not, the vast majority of your target audience members check their Facebook, Twitter, Pinterest, and YouTube accounts within a certain block of time every single day. Post outside of that block of time and you miss the eyeballs of the vast majority of your audience members.

Sounds good so far, right? Well, here's the problem: different audiences have different time preferences. How would you know? This is where experimentation comes in.

First, you're going to have to share your content randomly at different times of the day. As much as possible, share content every hour. Set your content automation tools to publish every hour. Let this run for about a week or two.

After the experimental period is over, check your stats. Facebook Insights, for example, will tell you when most of your page fans checked out your content. Armed with this information, you should set up your automated software to publish your content in a cluster to fit those optimal times.

For example, in the experimental stage, you're publishing one piece of content every hour. That's 24 pieces of content spread out over a full 24 hours. After you checked Facebook Insight, it turned out that 80% of your content views actually take place between 8:00 a.m. and 5:00 p.m. You then take those 24 posts and compress them within that 8:00 a.m. to 5:00 p.m. window.

This is how you publish in clusters. Forget time blocks outside of that time frame. This way, you maximize your chances of the right eyeballs seeing your content.

Special Notes for Twitter

If you are going to be publishing on Twitter, re-publish your content many times during the day at the most optimal time frame. Facebook Insight already told you that your content is being viewed within a specific time frame. Chances are, your Twitter fans have the same

social media viewing habits. Stick to that time frame.

Now, here's the secret. Set up your automated content publishing tools to tweet out your best content many times during that time frame, but you also have to rotate different hashtags. This way, you can reach different people looking for hashtags that are related to different subsegments of your niche.

Special Notes for Facebook

When publishing to your Facebook page, don't hesitate to publish original content that you have published before. Try to avoid publishing only once. Instead, you should sandwich or schedule this re-published successful content in between high

quality curated content.

This way, people get more exposure to your best content. Once they click through, you get yet another chance to recruit them to your mailing list.

Remember, when you share high-quality third-party content, you're not getting the traffic. You're building credibility, but you're not getting potential list members to your squeeze page. That's just not happening. When you share your own original content, you get a chance to recruit them to your squeeze page.

Keep this distinction in mind. This is the reason why you should re-publish your most successful content by interspersing it with top-rated curated content.

Chapter 13 - Scale Up Your Targeting

When you're publishing on Facebook and Twitter, you can use hashtags. This is definitely true with Instagram. Regardless of the platform, you're on, make sure you play around with how you categorize or tag your content.

In any niche, there are many different tags available. Experiment with these. See which tags get the most attention from the social media platform you're sharing a piece of content on.

Of course, you're not going to find the magical combination of hashtags overnight. That's not going to happen. This is one of those things that you're going to have to find out by doing it over a long period of time.

Still, when you run these experiments, a pattern should emerge. Sooner or later, you would discover that certain hashtags produce a lot more results than others. They draw a lot more eyeballs. They get a lot more attention. Most importantly, they get a lot more engagement. Stick with those.

Experiment with Tagging Niche-Focused Influencers

When you're doing research on hashtags on Twitter, for example, you would be able to find influencers that specialize in those hashtags. These people just love to post content related to certain topics. They use a narrow range of hashtags every time

they post. It seems that's all they focus on.

Find these people. Look at their content. Are people retweeting them a lot? Are they getting a lot of love for their content? Do they get a lot of engagement? Are people responding via Twitter? It should be fairly easy to see which accounts are influential in your niche and which aren't.

Don't just focus on how many followers they have. Instead, look at the total amount of engagement they get, and also pay attention to the ratio of followers they have to the number of accounts they follow.

For example, if I find Mike Smith to be a big poster in my niche because it seems that he just seems to rotate among the ten hashtags that are most relevant to my niche, I look at his followers in relation to the number of accounts he's following. If he's only following one person, yet he's being followed by 15,000 people, Mike Smith might be an influential person.

I say that he might be because I'm also going to have to look at the engagement levels of his posts. Are his posts getting a lot of retweets? Are a lot of people responding? Are a lot of people clicking the heart icon? If his content has these factors, then his account is probably worth following.

Most importantly, you should tag influential people on Twitter when you post. You use your most powerful hashtags and you mention them in your post. This can help you get on their radar. These people would be put on notice that you are also sharing content that is similar to the stuff that they are interested in.

If they check out your stuff and they like what they see, don't be surprised if they share your content with their following. Engage with them. Let them know about your questions or suggestions.

In fact, you should engage with them so much that you can possibly create a relationship where they would publish your guest posts if they're bloggers, or discuss whatever it is you're doing on their social media platforms.

At the very least, when you partner with them, they become part of your content distribution network. In fact, a lot of them can even get you interviewed on influential blogs in your niche.

Don't think that influencer engagement is simply restricted to tagging people. That's just the beginning. That's actually the tip of the iceberg. They can do so much more for you. You just have to continuously engage them and be social.

This doesn't mean that you have to kiss their butt. This doesn't mean that your stock response to all of their posts is, "Amazing post" or "Great post. I love it." That's not going to work.

That's not going to push the ball far enough. You have to actually engage. And oftentimes, this might seem like you're criticizing them. This might seem that you are offering a negative view, but you need to get their attention. You need to bring home the point that you actually know your stuff and that you are also credible in the same niche space.

That's how you get them to take you seriously. That's the kind of engagement that builds respect. Otherwise, you're just going to look like another member of the choir. They really don't have any incentive to interview you or post your guest content. Why should they? You're not really sharing any information or suggesting any points of view that *are* different or distinctive.

Experiment with Paid Traffic

Only after you have spent a lot of time drumming up free traffic from social media marketing should you even think of buying traffic. I know this sounds a bit extreme, but it's the absolute truth. Why? Well, in the beginning, you don't know when your target audience members will be reading your content. In the beginning, you don't know what their demographic breakdown looks like.

How many males compared to females are in your audience pool? Do males or females like certain types of content that you share? What are their age ranges? Where are they located?

I hope you see the big picture here. You have to use free traffic to do initial audience intelligence. Once you've got all these important insights, you can then start paying for Facebook ads and other platforms' ads.

If you start any earlier than this point, you probably would end up wasting your money. Study your statistics first. Pay close attention to audience patterns. Take out ads based on these patterns.

Chapter 14: Sell to Your List Differently

At this point, you have turned social media traffic into list members. Congratulate yourself. You've managed to do something the vast majority of social media marketers cannot do or, worse yet, don't even think about doing. It's quite an accomplishment.

Unfortunately, even at this point, it's still too easy to drop the ball. In fact, a lot of people who have mailing lists stay with one mailing list. They think that as long as people who visit their blogs sign up to their mailing list, they are good.

Well, at a certain level, they're correct. A certain percentage of those list members will buy affiliate products that you promote on your list. A certain fraction of your mailing list will buy your original products. Some may even visit your online store and buy merchandise.

But the problem here is that if you accept this scenario, you are settling for cents on the dollar. You really are. Don't you want to maximize the value of all the hard work, focus, and energy you invested in your venture? Wouldn't you want to maximize your return on effort?

If you want to get maximum results from your mailing list, you have to sell your list differently. There are really no two ways about it. Every other approach would lead to, at best, mediocre results, or, at worst, no results at all. Keep the following tips in mind.

Use Different Content on Your List

When people join your mailing list, chances are, they joined because they got exposed to some of your content.

They already know what you talk about. They are already familiar with the quality of your content. They understand the themes that you focus on. That's why it doesn't make any sense for you to feature the same exact content on your list.

Sure, you may make some changes—you might change the title, you might even switch things around—but people aren't dumb. They can see right through that. They can see that you are recycling content and feeding them stuff that they have probably seen before.

Do you think this kind of practice builds confidence? Do you believe that doing things this way will build trust? Of course, not. You have to use different content.

What kind of content will you have to use? Well, first of all, you already know what your most popular pieces of content are. Start with these.

No, I'm not talking about republishing them. I'm talking about analyzing them and seeing where the gaps are. Are there any questions that are left unanswered? Are there any questions that were raised by the answers that you gave in those popular pieces of content? These should be enough to get your mind going as to the kind of finely tuned, high-value content that you're going to be sharing on your list.

Remember, your updates are the ultimate reward to your list members. Sure, you may have positioned your squeeze page to reward subscribers with a premium, but once they downloaded that premium, they really have no other incentive to keep reading your emails. Do you see how that works?

So do yourself a big favor and make sure that the updated content you send is the reward. That's how you get people to open your emails and read your materials over and over again. Reward them for being on your list.

Don't drop your guard, don't take it easy, don't give in to laziness. This is your time to rise and shine. Everything else that happened before this just dressed rehearsal. This is it. This is where the rubber meets the road. And you better perform.

Use Premium Content

If you really want to hit the ball out of the park with your mailing list, send updates that really highlight how original the content is. How do you do this? Use social proof or case studies. These are testimonials of people that have taken your advice or who have experienced certain things that you talk about.

When people read these stories, they can't help but be engaged. They can't help but be absorbed into the narrative. These people sharing their testimonies are real flesh and blood human beings with real problems that your readers can relate to. That's the kind of compelling content that will take your list to a whole other level.

Why? Most of your competitors are just recycling their stuff. Sure, they're recycling their best stuff because that material is tried and proven, but they're not really distinguishing themselves. They're not really doing their brand any favors by taking the easy way out.

You have to commit to doing things differently. This is how you build loyalty around your content. Remember, when you're running a mailing list, your content is composed of the emails you send out. No more, no less.

Upsell, Upsell, Upsell

I can't say that word "upsell" enough. If you want your list to make money, you have to upsell. Now, you don't have to be a hero. You don't have to overdo this. You don't have to come off like some sort of super salesman.

If you're like most people, you know
how annoying pushy salespeople are. You probably will push back. You will probably tune them out and unsubscribe. I can't say I blame you. That's how most normal people respond to pushy salespeople.

By upsell, I am just telling you to send content that highlights a problem and a solution. That's all upselling is. You remind people of their range of problems and you remind them of certain solutions to them.

Now, of course, just like with most things in life, there are good solutions and even better ones. Your job is to send email updates that get people excited about finding a solution and laying out common solutions that are good but are not the best.

What you're doing here is you're drawing their attention to the very best solution to their problems. For example, if you run a social media marketing mailing list, you can tell people that creating picture quotes and videos from pictures is a great solution to their original content needs.

But an even better solution would be to automate these materials where people just click on images and all of a sudden a video is created. It saves a tremendous amount of time, effort, energy, and most importantly, the created video would then automatically be uploaded to their social media accounts.

That's the kind of distinction between "good enough" solutions and "obviously superior" solutions. That's how you upsell people to your list. You're still providing value, you're still answering their questions, you're still addressing their needs, but you're laying out a range of options.

They can try to do things on their own or try to do things the way most people handle the problem, or they can try something else. When they look at that "something else," that's when you sell your affiliate product, your original product, or your service. Regardless of how you do it, you need to upsell, upsell, upsell.

I wish I could tell you that this was easy. I wish I could tell you that this is just a simple matter of laying out some alternatives and then playing up the best solution. The best solution, of course, pays you a commission and you make money off each sale.

Unfortunately, it's not that easy and it's not that simple. Here's the reason. When people join your mailing list, they actually have different motivations. Some people are there because they just want to get the freebie, but they're too lazy to unsubscribe.

You cannot really get rid of these people. These people don't open your emails. They cannot be bothered with reading your emails. They really don't do you much good. In fact, they can harm you because if there are enough of these list squatters on your list, your mailing list provider will charge you more money at the end of every month.

You have to actively filter your list based on open rates so you can get rid of these individuals. Again, you cannot eliminate them entirely, but you can minimize their numbers.

Other people are initially excited about your mailing list, but for some reason, they stopped reading your emails. Even others constantly check your emails, and they really love what you have to share, but the problem is, they feel that your premium offers are simply too expensive.

Now, let me clue you in on a secret. When somebody tells you that whatever you're offering is "too expensive" or "too unaffordable," what they're really trying to say is that you haven't completely sold them on it yet.

Alternatively, you haven't completely filtered them yet. Either they're not motivated enough or you did not give them enough reasons to be motivated. Regardless, they're still on the fence. You need to push them off the fence.

Expert salespeople know this because, in the big scheme of things, there is no such thing as "unaffordable."

If you talk to somebody and you convince that person that they absolutely need to buy your product, there's really no difference between a $10 product and a $1,000 product. They will get that product because you have elevated their perception of that product to the realm of need.

People take care of their needs first. Their wants are often left at the back burner. I hope you understand this. I hope you get this. It's not because your affiliate product is too expensive in absolute terms. Instead, it's because you have failed to either qualify the prospect or make your case.

And this is why simply upselling by itself is not going to work. You have to take the next step, which I'm going to describe below.

Use the $1 List Filtration Method

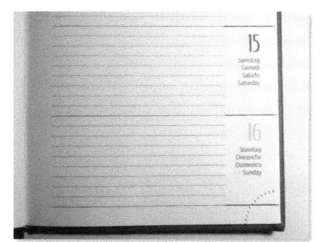

You have to filter your list members into two groups: interested people and interested people who buy. These are two totally different groups of people.

Now, please understand that just because people open your emails religiously, it doesn't necessarily mean that they would buy from you. Like I said above, maybe you did not present your case properly. Maybe you did not qualify them properly.

This $1 list filtration technique that I'm going to teach you enables you to filter your list members properly. What you would do is, instead of trying to upsell people to $19.95, $34.95, $349.50, or any other similarly priced products, everything that you're going to be selling on your general list will be priced $1. No more, no less.

By general list, I'm talking about the list all people who sign up to your mailing list get on. This is your default list. I want you to treat this general list as your starting list. This is kind of like the vast, unfiltered, generic mass of people who are interested in your brand.

When you upsell people using $1 offers, you enable people to segregate themselves based on their motivations. These are people who are motivated enough to spend $1. In other words, they see the value in your content and they are willing to put their money where their mouth is.

Now, here's the secret. There's really very little distance between paying $1 for something and paying $100 for something. This is a lesson I learned first hand.

When I first tried this, I thought the only people that will get on my dollar list are cheapskates. These are misers. In the back of my mind, I thought that they're just not going to buy big-ticket items. Boy, was I proven wrong.

If somebody is able to psychologically hurdle the distance between zero and $1, they can given enough exposure and enough content, hurdle the difference between $1 and $100. This is not theory, nor is it speculation. I see this all the time with my own two eyes.

Your job is to filter your general list. You're basically telling people, when you run these $1 offers, to prove to you whether they are just interested or truly interested. This is a self-segregating mechanism. Use it.

People who sign up for your general list are interested in quality content. That's what they're there for. But only a fraction of them would actually be willing to pay money. You make your money off this "golden fraction." You use your buyer's list to make real money.

Again, you have to sell to your list differently. This applies to your two types of mailing lists as well. Your general list, they get quality information that is distinctive like social proof and case studies along with upselling messages. Your buyer's list, on the other hand, get more in-depth material with higher value upsells.

Again, if somebody's willing to go from zero to $1, you have a tremendous opportunity to get that person to go from $1 to $100, $1,000, or whatever amount you want. Now, keep in mind that the higher the dollar value, the lower the conversion rate, but you get the point.

You have to get people to segregate themselves based on their readiness, willingness, and eagerness to buy. And since $1 is essential "friction-free," this list filtration method works like a charm.

Chapter 15 - Reinvest Your Profits the Right Way

By this point, the $1 filtration method has enabled you to make a decent chunk of cash every single month from social media traffic. The next step is to create a business.

At this point, you might be feeling that you're just engaged in a hobby. It's a well-paid hobby, but still a hobby nonetheless. This too can be a trap. This can hold you back from the great success that you could otherwise achieve with social media traffic.

How do you turn the information that I shared with you into a platform for a business that can withstand the test of time? Simple: reinvest your profits the right way.

Move into Other Niches after You Master Your System

This training helps you identify your target niche. I've also given you the techniques to do well in that niche using social media traffic. Once you've made quite a bit of money on your niche and this money comes in month after month, you have to think big. You have to look into other niches that are related to your current niche.

This thinking is actually pretty straightforward. If you have already mastered your niche to the point that you're making automatic income month after month, then you can apply the same system to other niches that are closely related to the one you're in.

This is how you scale up your business. Instead of just one stream of cash, you build many different streams of cash based on the system that you mastered.

You know what hashtags to target, you know what kind of content gets eyeballs, you know how to present information on social media, you know how to promote a mailing list. These and many others form part of your system. It really would be a shame to restrict that system to just one niche.

Once you've mastered those, find niches related to those and grow into these other fields. Highly successful list marketers don't just operate one list. They operate dozens. And this translates to six, if not seven-figure incomes year after year. If they can do it, so can you.

Buy More Targeted Traffic after You Find Out What Works

Once you have discovered the type of content marketing strategy on Facebook that works, you can buy targeted traffic. How? Use Facebook's lookalike technology to target people who share the same interest profile as your existing audience.

This is what's so awesome about Facebook. This is also what gets them into all sorts of hot water.

Believe it or not, accept it or not, Facebook is spying on you the moment you log in to the platform. It pays attention to what you like, it pays attention to what you comment on, it pays attention to what your friends like, and it makes all sorts of predictions regarding your behavior and your interests. Accordingly, if you like certain topics, it creates an interesting profile.

Facebook's lookalike audience technology enables you to find people who haven't visited your Facebook page who share the same interest profile as your current fans. Talk about an amazing technology. Take advantage of this. It enables you to show your brand in front of eyeballs who are more likely to appreciate it.

Invest in More Original Content

You might want to invest in original content. If you're already making a decent profit from your current system, you might want to take things to the next level and add a lot more value to the lives of people following your brand on different social media platforms as well as in your blog or website with original content.

Now, This doesn't mean that you have to roll up your sleeves and write everything yourself. You can hire professional writers to do this. Thanks to global outsourcing, you can get high-quality original content from places like ozki.org without it costing you an arm and a leg. You can get high-quality content that truly engages your audiences without it killing your profit margin.

Invest in More Content Updates

This advice really flows from the previous point I raised. If you're going to be investing in more original content, automatically, you will be investing in more content updates. You will have a lot more original materials to share.

These two actions go together. Regardless, you need to step it up in terms of content updates so you can pack a lot more value.

Invest in Your Original Products

When you're starting out setting up this system I teach you in this training, you probably would be focused on affiliate products. You get an affiliate from an affiliate program, you market that links on your email updates. When somebody clicks on that link and buys something, you get a commission. Pretty straightforward, very simple.

Well, if you really want to make a lot of money, you have to turn your back on affiliate marketing. You really do. Instead, you have to sell your own stuff. The reason why you need to do this really boils down to control. When you are selling other people's materials, you are at the mercy of their squeeze page, their landing page, and ultimately, the quality of their product.

What if their product sucks? What if their sales page converts only a fraction of the people it could otherwise have converted? You lose out. That's the bottom line. If you want to maximize your control over your income, you need to invest in your own original products.

Thankfully, outsourcing is always available to you. You can outsource to professional companies like ozki.org and other specialized content producers to help you produce high-quality original materials for cents on the dollar.

Sell Your Own Video-Based Membership courses

The main problem with product sales online is, by and large, you're selling the item once. Somebody clicks the "buy" button, they pay, they get access to the download link, and that's the end of the story. They already have the product. They can enjoy it, they can throw it away, they can do whatever they want with it.

But the transaction only took place once. Wouldn't it be awesome if people keep sending you money every month? Wouldn't it be great if you get recurring income? Well, that's exactly what you can enjoy when you sell your own video-based membership courses.

For example, if you have a gardening blog, you can set up a video-based course where you teach people the ins and outs of garden cultivation. Every single month, each member's PayPal account or credit card account is billed a certain amount. You don't have to lift a finger. And this goes on month after month after month until they cancel.

The best part? You shot the videos once, yet you make money off of them month after month. How awesome is that? This is called passive income.

And the great thing about this is that you don't have to stick with video. It can be any kind of membership. Maybe you can give them access to pictures. Maybe you can give them access to files or even software, it doesn't matter.

What they're paying for is the right to download that material month after month. This is the key. Recurring income should be your ultimate goal. This is how you maximize your effort. You're putting in less work while getting more money out of the system.

Unfortunately, this is not something that you can master getting out of the gate. It also doesn't happen overnight. You have to pay your dues by doing the other steps above first.

Conclusion

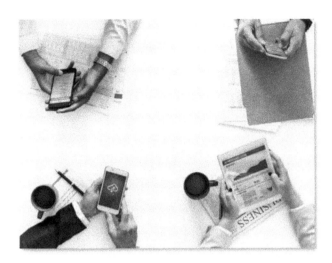

Social media marketing confuses a lot of people. It definitely leads to a lot of dead ends if you let its myths get the better of you. This training shines a light on one effective way of using social media exposure to turn social media reach into cold, hard cash in your bank account.

While I'm not claiming that these steps are easy, they are doable. You just need to follow instructions, you need to conduct experiments, and focus on what works.

The key here is to use this information to fit your particular set of circumstances to produce practical, actionable steps that you can use to earn a truly passive income. Don't move one step ahead until you've mastered the previous step.

Now that you have all the information that you need to succeed, please understand that none of this will make you rich if you let it stay in your head. Not in a million years. You have to take action on them. You have to get that sense of urgency you need to make this information a reality. The longer it stays in your head, the less likely your finances will change.

Give yourself a deadline. Commit to firm start date. Once that date comes, start. You don't have to be a hero, you don't have to hit a home run the first time you step up to the plate. As long as you're making a small step forward, that is good enough.

Why? A small step forward is still a step forward. You have to keep doing it. You have to take step after step. It doesn't matter what side of the bed you woke upon, it doesn't matter what you're feeling—none of that matters. What matters is you stick to the plan.

If you're able to commit and focus, you will succeed. I wish you nothing but the greatest success. Thank you for watching this training.